Watercolour by J. A. Hodgson *'Bassenthwaite from Keswick 1849'.*
From Keswick Museum Collections.

Contents

Before you begin. . .

Our first three trails begin at the Moot Hall in the Market Square.

Numbers refer to those shown on the map at the back of the booklet.

With thanks to Keswick Civic Society (which no longer exists but produced a similar earlier publication) and George Bott (Keswick's local historian who provided much of the original information).

Trail 1: From Pack Horse to The Age of Steam

(Allow 45 minutes plus additional time, if you wish, for a visit to the exhibitions and cafe at Keswick Museum).

Start at the Moot Hall Information Centre on the Market Square and head out with the ROYAL OAK HOTEL on your left. Turn left into Station Street and turn into the arcade on the left. Look on the right for the plaque detailing the history of the Hotel, including some of its clientele.

1 THE ROYAL OAK: This ancient inn, as the plaque records, has been visited by many famous people, including Southey and Wordsworth, and for centuries was a coaching inn where post for the town was delivered.

In the last shop on the right, some of the magnificent stained glass windows from the hotel dining room are still visible, featuring Wordsworth, Coleridge, Southey and John Peel.

WW1 memorial stained glass window now on display at Keswick Museum but originally designed for the Royal Oak Hotel in 1929.
From Keswick Museum Collections.

Continue to:

② PACKHORSE COURT: Turn right and note the plaque just before you
turn right on to Standish Street. This was one of a number of yards
found on both sides of the market place from mediaeval times
onward. Originally, Main Street was divided into 'burgage' plots with
timber-framed houses and gardens or orchards behind them. By the
eighteenth century stone had replaced timber and the long garden
strips were occupied by small buildings and workshops – compact
communities of cottage industries many of which remained into the
twentieth century.

In recent years the yards have been much altered and little remains to show
their early pattern and function. From Keswick Museum collections.

Walk up Standish Street to rejoin Station Street and turn left. Look across
the street at the shop and office of:

③ THE KESWICK REMINDER: The town's own weekly newspaper, first
published in 1897; a rarity these days in a town of less than six
thousand residents.

Continue a few metres to the junction of four roads. Cross by the traffic lights and the pedestrian refuge to the:

④ WAR MEMORIAL: On the back is a copper tablet in memory of the employees of the Cockermouth, Keswick and Penrith Railway who lost their lives in the 1914-18 War.

As you walk down Station Road, note the plaques and the Frances Rolleston drinking fountain (erected 1865) on the right-hand wall. The fountain was restored in 2000 by the Civic Society. When you reach the BRIDGE look left downstream.

Curling on the River Greta at Silver Bridge with the Pavilion behind c. 1900. From Keswick Museum collections.

⑤ FROM THE BRIDGE: On your left is a block of flats, Riverside Lodge, opened in 1989. It occupies the site of the Queen of the Lakes Pavilion, built in 1894 and a popular venue for dances, whist drives, plays and other social events. The wooden walkway leads to the Youth Hostel, once a hotel and opened as a hostel in 1933. Further on are several more blocks of flats, some converted from the original mills, including a 19th century pencil mill.

Cross the bridge and enter Fitz Park on the right and skirt the public bowling green and turn left to the park kiosk. 'Fitz' means water meadow and the park has indeed flooded seriously in 2005, 2009 and 2015. You can find a guide to the trees in the of Fitz Park in Keswick Museum.

6 Opposite the kiosk is a memorial bust of **SIR JOHN BANKES (see trail 2).**

Continue through the large wrought iron gates with their gilded dedication to the philanthropist Henry Irwin Jenkinson whose efforts were largely responsible for the creation of Fitz Park.

Turn right and continue straight ahead on a footpath uphill passing the leisure centre to your left. At the back of the leisure centre, turn right up on to:

7 The platform of the former **RAILWAY STATION:** This connects directly to the Keswick Hotel. The Cockermouth, Keswick Penrith Railway opened fully in 1865 and closed in 1972. It was key to the growth of Keswick as a tourist destination. Retrace your steps past the leisure centre to Station Road and notice the sweeping drive to the large, former railway hotel.

Keswick signal box and station c. 1900. From Keswick Museum collections.

Back down Station Road on the right is:

8 **KESWICK MUSEUM:** Built in 1897, it was founded by the Keswick Literary and Scientific Society (still alive and active as the Keswick Lecture Society) to house their collections. These were started in 1873 and were displayed for some years in the Moot Hall. The 'Art Gallery' was added in 1906.

The museum now hosts exhibitions, activities and events about the landscape, people, heritage and culture of the Keswick area including *Keswick in 100 Curious Objects*. One of the objects featured is the Musical Stones of Skiddaw or Rock & Steel Band, made from local stone… probably Britain's first Rock Band!

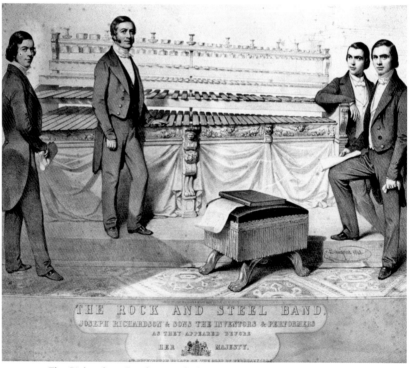

The Richardson Brothers with the Musical Stones, as they appeared before Queen Victoria in 1848. From Keswick Museum collections.

Trail 2: Keswick Town and Crosthwaite Village
(Allow 1 hour - 1¹/2 hours).

(9) **The MOOT HALL:** The origins of this building are obscure. As early as 1571, there is a reference to a Court House in the Market Place. Tradition suggests it was built in 1695 with materials from the Earl of Derwentwater's family mansion on Lord's Island, Derwentwater. The present building dates from 1813 and has been used as a manor courthouse, a butter and fruit market, a prison, a museum and a town hall. Its one-handed clock (probably 1601) may be seen on the west end above the steps.

Cross the road to the the building next to John Young's Antiques shop:

(10) **The HOME OF SIR JOHN BANKES:** Born at nearby Castlerigg in 1589, he was educated at Crosthwaite School and Queen's College, Oxford. In 1641, he was appointed Lord Chief Justice of the Common Pleas (from which the Pub on Bank St gets its name) and a Privy Councillor the following year. He died in Oxford in 1644 and was buried in the chapel of Christ's Church College. He left money for the Bankes' charitable trust in Keswick and for a poorhouse.

Go through the arch by the side of Young's shop (King's Head Court) to see:

(11) **JONATHAN OTLEY'S COTTAGE:** 'up the steps': Born near Grasmere in 1766, Otley came to Keswick in 1791 and worked as a watch and clock repairer. Much in demand as a geologist, meteorologist and guide, he was consulted by eminent scientists and in 1823 wrote one of the first reliable guide books to the Lake District.

A Keswick Yard and Otley's steps by Tom Wilson, 1900.
From Keswick Museum collections.

Have a look at the other yards as you walk down the street (one below the Golden Lion Inn has a good example of an original wall) to the last building on the right before the road:

Keswick Yard c. 1890. From Keswick Museum collections.

12 **THE POORHOUSE :** The entrance of Bank Street was the site of Sir John Bankes' Poorhouse for the parish of Crosthwaite (Keswick did not have a church and therefore parish until 1838) . He left £200 for the building and money "to raise a stock of Wool, Flax, Hemp, Thread, Iron and other necessary wear and stuff to set the poor on work who were born in the parish of Crosthwaite". There were 30 inmates in a report of 1777. In 1838, the Union Workhouse was established in Cockermouth to take the poor from 47 parishes, including Keswick and Crosthwaite, although this poorhouse remained for some time after this.

The arched entrance to the old Poorhouse with the council offices behind c. 1890.
From Keswick Museum collections.

Across the road on the opposite corner are the:

13 COUNCIL OFFICES: The building (1864) was originally the Cumberland Union Bank, hence the name 'Bank Street'. Keswick Urban District Council became Keswick Town Council in 1974 and still has offices and a council chamber in the building. Note the clock which was given in 1932 by the P.U.P.S. (the Pushing Young People's Society, founded in 1928). Also on Bank Street was the Victorian Post Office (now a shop), Police Station and Courthouse (now a pub).

Cross the street and walk further down Main Street to the entrance of:

14 MUSEUM SQUARE :
In the late eighteenth and early nineteenth centuries Peter Crosthwaite's Museum was sited here. It was one of the main attractions of the town.

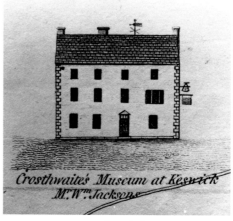

Crosthwaite's Museum at Keswick
Mr Wm Jackson's

Details from Crosthwaite's map of Bassenthwaite. From Keswick Museum Collections.

Born near Keswick in 1735, Crosthwaite served as a naval captain deterring Malay pirates for the East India Company and later as a Customs Officer at Blyth, before retiring to Keswick in 1780 to assemble and exhibit a large collection of both local natural history and curious foreign objects. He was an ingenious inventor, a fine cartographer and quite a business entrepreneur. He died in 1808.
A few pieces of his collection remain in the current Keswick Museum.

Re-cross Main Street and continue past the bottom of Stanger Street, named after a well-known local family of 19th century philanthropists. If time permits walk to the top of Stanger Street to see on the left GRETA HAMLET, built in 1909 in the style of the Garden City movement.
The impetus for development came from some far sighted, philanthropic local businessmen. Returning to Main Street, the narrow opening across the road leads (Heads Lane) to the Library.

Staying on the right side of Main Street, past the Co-op supermarket, is:

15 CROSTHWAITE PARISH ROOM: Distinguished by the ancient bell on the gable end. The room was officially opened in November 1879 as a memorial to the Rev G. G. Goodwin, vicar of Crosthwaite Church in 1878. Canon Rawnsley and his wife Edith ran carving and metalwork classes in the winter here from 1884-1894. This was the beginning of the Keswick School of Industrial Arts. Ten years later they moved to their own building (see 19).

Immediately past the Parish Room is the Rawnsley Centre and the original site of:

16 KESWICK SCHOOL:
This co-educational day and boarding school was opened in 1898, largely financed by the generosity of the Hewetson family and supported by Canon Rawnsley. The school has now relocated (see 27). The site now serves as a conference centre - Rawnsley Hall and a small housing development.

On the hill behind the former school is:

Robert Southey aged 31 by John Opie. From Keswick Museum collections.

17 GRETA HALL: Built about 1800, this house was the former home first of Samuel Taylor Coleridge and then Robert Southey, poet laureate, who lived here for forty years. Many famous literary personalities visited Greta Hall - the Wordsworths, Charles Lamb, William Hazlitt, Shelley and Sir Walter Scott. From 1872 to 1887, it was a girls' school: in 1909 it was rented to Keswick School headmaster as a girls' boarding house. In 1921, it was bought by the governors of the school and remained a girls' boarding house until 1994. It is now privately owned.

Southey's first wife Edith was sister to Coleridge's wife. The Southeys moved to Keswick in 1803 following the death of their first daughter, Margaret, for Edith Southey's comfort. Coleridge did not stay long in Keswick, but left his family at Greta Hall in Southey's care. Southey wrote long, epic poems which are not well remembered today. He also wrote histories – of Brazil, Portugal and Nelson. His poem *The Cataract of Lodore,* a shape poem, was written for his children.

Continue on the main road to the bridge. On the right is the site of the former:

18 CUMBERLAND PENCIL WORKS: The current buildings were erected in 1937. It is claimed that the first graphite pencils ever made were produced in Keswick following the discovery of graphite (locally known as wad) at Seathwaite in Borrowdale, in the 1500s. Originally a cottage industry, pencil making expanded in the mid 1800s when the first factory began production. Several firms operated in the 1800s and early 1900s but today the Cumberland Pencil Company has re-located to a purpose built factory in West Cumbria. The whole site is in the early stages of a planned redevelopment.

The interior of one of Keswick's pencil factories in the nineteenth century.
From Keswick Museum collections.

Over the bridge on the left is the former:

19 KESWICK SCHOOL OF INDUSTRIAL ARTS: The school opened here in April 1894 (see also 15), the brainchild of Canon Rawnsley and his wife Edith. It was a centre for training local craftsmen, producing high quality articles in copper, brass, silver and, from 1931, 'staybrite' stainless steel. The products stamped K.S.I.A. are much sought after today. Note the inscription "The loving eye and patient hand shall work with joy and bless the land" which was the motto of the school. The school ran for 100 years until 1984.

Interior of Keswick School of Art.

Keswick School of Arts Showroom and jewellery designs by Atholl Weeks, KSIA director from 1920 – 1951. Photo: by permission of private lender.

Continue along Main Street opposite a row of cottages, one of which is:

20 **PORCH COTTAGE:** From 1894, for nearly thirty years, this cottage and the adjacent Ruskin Cottage were the home of the Ruskin Linen Industry, a small but thriving venture inspired by John Ruskin and started by Miss Marion Twelves in Langdale in 1883. She came to Keswick in 1889 and under her guidance and expertise products of the industry won many awards and were sold world-wide.

Photograph of Marion Twelves outside Porch Cottage.
From Keswick Museum collections.

21 Over the wall on your right are the restored **RETTING STEPS:** This was where the flax was soaked in the River Greta to break down the cellulose coating and expose the fibres. Note, too, the drinking fountain, one of several erected in the town by Samuel Ladyman in the 1870s. The new wall and glass barriers here were erected as part of Keswick's flood defences in 2009 but were over-topped in 2015 flooding.

Immediately across the road is the site of the old Joiners' Arms, as the wall plaque shows and

22 **TOLL BAR COTTAGE:** This was once the house where road tolls were collected. In 1761, an Act of Parliament set up Turnpike Trusts, responsible for the road from Kendal to Cockermouth via Keswick. Each of the routes in and out of the town had its own tollhouse, of which this is an example.

TOLL BAR. HIGH HILL. KESWICK. 1846. TOM WILSON.

Drawing by Tom Wilson. From Keswick Museum collections.

The building just past the Retting Steps is:

23 ST HERBERT CENTRE: Financed by James Stanger in 1833 and described in a contemporary newspaper as: one of the most splendid schools in this part of the kingdom as regards architectural beauty, this Sunday School attracted some 350 children. On weekdays it was used to teach girls reading, knitting, sewing and cookery.
As Crosthwaite C of E school, it served the community as a school for girls and infants until it closed in 1993.

Engraving of St. Herberts Centre when a school in mid 19th century.
From Keswick Museum collections.

Just round the corner is:

24 QUAKER COTTAGE: In 1685 Hugh Tickell bought a house and orchard for use by local Friends, which was replaced by a new Meeting House in 1715. Later three cottages were built inside its walls and alterations in this century converted these into the present Quaker Cottage. From 1920 the Friends met in a Meeting House in Church Street. The new premises in Tithebarn Street were opened in 1994.

Cross the junction to the:

25 CATHOLIC CHURCH of Our Lady and St Charles: In 1926, Father Stephen Dawes, a monk from Ampleforth, bought a plot of land here and commissioned an architect to design a church. It was officially opened in July 1928, finally completed in 1965, and fully consecrated in November 1972. This church is built from Threlkeld granite.

Continue along the main road until you reach the last bungalow on the right hand side. Turn right and then immediately left.

As you walk towards the church, look right. The buildings on the hill are the current:

26 KESWICK SCHOOL: Here in 1951 a secondary modern mixed school was opened with boarding facilities for pupils from remote areas. In 1995 it combined with the grammar school to become a comprehensive for 11-18yr olds and in 2011 an academy. The original building formerly belonged to the Stanger family.

At the end of the road is

27 CROSTHWAITE OLD SCHOOL: Possibly founded in the fourteenth century by Sir Thomas de Eskhead, the school was certainly in existence in 1571 as a free grammar school for boys. When Keswick School was formed, it became a boys' elementary and then a mixed primary. In 1974, it was closed but in 2004 the building was modernised and enlarged and once again used by Keswick School.

Watercolour of Crosthwaite Church by Lucy Gipps, 1863.
From Keswick Museum collections.

28 CROSTHWAITE CHURCH: Tradition has it that St Kentigern, later Bishop of Glasgow, turned aside from a journey to Wales in 553 and set up a cross in the forest clearing. It is said that a church was built here in 1181. Over the centuries, alterations and additions have been made - a rebuilding in the sixteenth century and a major restoration in 1844 financed by James Stanger.

Don't miss the panoramic viewfinder and the graves of Southey and Jonathan Otley in the churchyard and the reredos made by KSIA. Canon Hardwicke Drummond Rawnsley was vicar of Crosthwaite from 1883 to 1917 and co-founder of the National Trust.

Canon Hardwicke Drummond Rawnsley. From Keswick Museum collections.

Crosthwaite Old Vicarage by Lucy Gipps. From Keswick Museum collections.

Trail 3: Down to Derwentwater

(Allow 1 hour - 1¹/₂ hours).

Leave the Market Square past the Royal Oak Hotel and bear right on to St John's Street.

29 **GEORGE HOTEL:** Reputedly the oldest inn in Keswick, it has associations with graphite or 'black lead' smuggling and Sir John Ratcliffe - read the plaque by the front door and look in to see their collection of photos and artefacts.

The George Hotel c. 1920. From Keswick Museum collections.

Immediately opposite is the:

30 **DERWENT CLUB:** The site of the 'Governor's House' built in the 1730s. Edward Stephenson (1691 - 1768), an employee of the East India Company, was appointed Governor of Bengal in 1728 - for less than two days. He retired to Keswick, a wealthy man, and is buried under the altar in Crosthwaite Church.

About 200 metres further along St John's St at the top of the hill, the first turning to the left is Church Street. On the corner is a building which was

31 **ST JOHN'S LIBRARY:** It was built in 1849 by the Rev Frederick Myers, first vicar of St John's Church from 1838 to 1851. Upstairs was the Battersby Hall, a lecture room named after Myers' successor, the Rev Thomas Dundas Harford-Battersby.

Crossing the road, walk up the lane next to the church. Alongside is the building that until 1993 was

32 **ST JOHN'S SCHOOL:** Built in 1840 as a Sunday School, it was also used for teaching during the week. It has undergone several alterations in construction and use over the years and has now been converted into five dwellings.

St John's School Infants c. 1900. From Keswick Museum collections.

33 **ST JOHN'S CHURCH:** The building was financed by John Marshall, Lord of the Manor, former MP for Leeds and a member of a family which owned considerable property in the Lake District. It was opened in 1838 and has been extensively enlarged since then. John Marshall is buried in the nave of the church. In 1875, the vicar of St John's, the Rev Canon Harford Battersby, founded the Keswick Convention with the help of Robert Wilson of Broughton near Cockermouth.

The Convention Tent.   *Keswick.*

Postcard of the Eskin Street convention site, from Keswick Museum collections.
This annual assembly of Christians of all denominations is still held in July each
year welcoming thousands of visitors to the town.

Visit the grave of Sir Hugh Walpole on the terrace overlooking the lake and
the fells of Borrowdale.

Rejoin the lane and turn left down a sloping alleyway to the road.
Turn sharp right - note the outside steps on the first cottage - and continue
past:

34 **GEORGE FISHER'S:** From 1887 to 1967, this was home to The
Abraham Brothers' photographic business. George and Ashley were
pioneer rock climbers, responsible for many Lake District first ascents,
and also pioneering photographers. See the plaque on the wall.

Continue down Lake Road and walk through the underpass. Go through the gate directly ahead into:

35 **HOPE PARK:** The land was donated to the town in 1925 by Sir Percy Hope, a Keswick resident with a distinguished record of public service, local and national. It now has games, golf and a café.

The land at Hope Park was previously an area for the grazing of horses which were used to transport charabancs from Keswick Railway Station to the various hotels in the town. The Park was opened as a golf course on the 27th May 1927 and visited by Prince Edward in 1927 (pictured here with Sir Percy Hope). From Keswick Museum collections.

Walk through the park bearing left and rejoin the road leading to the lake. On the left is the:

36 **THEATRE BY THE LAKE:** The theatre opened in 1999 replacing the 'Blue Box' which occupied the site for many years. The 'Blue Box' was originally a post war travelling theatre which settled in the car park by the lake in 1975 (having failed its MOT!). A year round programme of repertory and visiting productions has made it into a major cultural feature for Cumbria.

Walk to the lake and boat landings where the foreshore area and the road towards Friars Crag was restored in 2009. Further along look for a Plaque in memory of Canon Rawnsley a dedicated lover of the Lake District and co-founder of the National Trust. Immediately opposite is:

37 **DERWENT ISLAND:** In the 1780s it was owned by Joseph Pocklington, an eccentric from a Nottinghamshire banking family, who built several follies on the island and organised annual regattas, with mock battles using live cannon. The island is now owned by the National Trust and the house is tenanted. It is open to the public on several days in the summer.

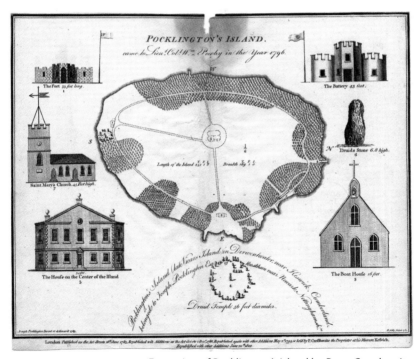

Engraving of Pocklington's Island by Peter Crosthwaite.
From Keswick Museum collections.

A little further on (right) is a short side path to the:

38 **RUSKIN MEMORIAL:** Unveiled in October 1900, this monument commemorates John Ruskin, who had many associations with Keswick. Apart from the early visit mentioned on the stone, he started his extensive collection of minerals here (now in Keswick Museum) and spent part of his honeymoon at the Royal Oak Hotel.
He once said "Keswick was a place almost too beautiful to live in".

Return to the main path and walk a few metres further to:

39 **FRIARS' CRAG:** Traditionally thought to be the place from which pilgrims embarked to visit St Herbert's Island (the wooded island in front). St Herbert lived as a hermit on the island in the seventh century, and was a disciple of St Cuthbert of Lindisfarne.

Ruskin described the view as one of the three most beautiful scenes in Europe. If the lake is low, look on the left-hand side of the Crag for the marker stones showing the previous low water levels.

View of Friars Crag by Joseph Brown of Keswick, c.1870, showing L to R Friars' Crag, Walla Crag and St Herbert's Island. From Keswick Museum collections.

4: Stretch your legs: 4 ideas for going a little further afield

These four locations are very rewarding. We have only provided a brief guide, so we recommend using Ordnance Survey Map OL4 and calling into the National Trust shop at Derwentwater foreshore (by the jetties) for guides to their waymarked trails.

40 CASTLEHEAD: Only accessible by foot. This fantastic view point was one of the eight 'viewing stations' recommended by Thomas West in his 1778 *'Guide to the Lakes'.* The short, steep climb provides a view of the length of Derwentwater. From the National Trust shop at Derwentwater foreshore, walk south for about 100 metres and then turn left along a narrow footpath, up through Cockshot Wood. Continue straight ahead to the Borrowdale Road. The hill ahead of you is Castlehead. Cross the road and follow a winding, sometimes muddy, path up hill to the summit. It is about half an hour from the jetties to the summit.

View from Castlehead today. © Keswick Museum.

41 CASTLERIGG STONE CIRCLE: To drive to the stone circle, head out of Keswick on the Penrith Road, turning left towards the A66 and Penrith, and then almost immediately turn right for the steep lane (Eleventrees) signposted to Castlerigg Stone Circle and Climbing Wall. Or you can walk the driving route in approximately one hour. For a pleasant longer route, walk via Springs Road, Castlerigg Farm, across the A591, and along Castle Lane to the stone circle.

This is one of the earliest of the British stone circles, dating from the Neolithic period, about 3000 BC. The view of the surrounding mountains and valleys is truly spectacular. The circle has never been fully excavated and its purpose is not clear, but it has a discernable entrance way and an unusual rectangular inner area. It is maintained by English Heritage and the National Trust. How many stones can you count?

Castlerigg Stone Circle today. © Keswick Museum.

42 LATRIGG: Climb the winding path up Keswick's nearest and, easiest Wainwright fell for a five mile return walk with spectacular views. Alternatively, there is a narrow road from Applethwaite to the small Gale Road car park, about ¾ of the way up.
Latrigg is one of the five foothills of Skiddaw, 'Keswick's Mountain'. Celebrationary beacons have been lit on Skiddaw over the centuries, with parties such as the one Wordsworth and Southey attended to celebrate the victory at Waterloo in 1815. It was one of the first fells to be climbed regularly by tourists and there used to be a refreshment hut in the summer months on Jenkin Hill, a little higher than Latrigg.

Next Page: *Lake Derwentwater* by Thomas Heatherley (1824-1913) with Skiddaw in the distance. From Keswick Museum collections.

43 **PORTINSCALE AND THE WESTERN SHORE OF DERWENTWATER:**
A mile or so from the centre of town, on a footpath across the
meadows and over the River Derwent is the village of Portinscale.
Alternatively, take the launch from the shore by the theatre.

Until the 1960s the main road to Cockermouth ran through the village
and it is the gateway to the western edge of Derwentwater. Here, a
number of notable country houses were built in the nineteenth
century: **Fawe Park,** 1858, and **Lingholm** in the 1870s – both holiday
destinations of Beatrix Potter who is said to have used for inspiration:
Catbells (Mrs Tiggywinkle), St Herbert's Island (Squirrel Nutkin) and
Fawe Park (Benjamin Bunny). **Hawse End** was home to Catherine
Marshall, a notable suffragist, working first in Keswick and then, after
the defeat of the 1910 Suffrage Bill, in London. In the 1920s Hugh
Walpole, the author, converted a bungalow called **Brackenburn,**
found further along the road to Grange, and lived there on and off
until his death in 1941. He housed his enormous library and art
collection in a study he built over the garage. On a private road in
Portinscale near the marinas, are two beautiful Arts and Crafts houses:
High Moss and **Little Ellers,** designed by W. H. Ward – an assistant to
Sir Edwin Lutyens - with landscaped gardens and stunning views.

March by National Union of Women's Suffrage Societies in 1918 at Greta Bridge.
From Keswick Museum collections.

Further Information

Websites:

Keswick Museum: http://keswickmuseum.org.uk/

KTA: http://www.keswick.org/

Cumbria Archives service: http://www.cumbria.gov.uk/archives/

Historic England Listed Building and Scheduled Ancient Monument search: https://historicengland.org.uk/listing/the-list/map-search

Listed Buildings (2015)

Grade 1:
Greta Hall Main Street

Grade 2*:
Church of St John St John's Street
Church of St Kentigern (Crosthwaite Parish Church) Church Lane
Moot Hall Main Street

Grade 2:
10-15, Borrowdale Road
123 and 125, Main Street
17-23, St John's Street
18, High Hill
2, Eskin Street
25, St John's Street
3, Penrith Road
3-6, High Hill
36-50, St John's Street
4 and 6, Derwent Street
4 and 6, Eskin Street
8 and 10, Eskin Street
85-91, Main Street
Balustrading, Urns, and Terrace Wall to Garden on North Side of Castlerigg Manor Ambleside Road
Bank Tavern Main Street
Brigham Forge Cottages Forge Lane
Calvert's Bridge Penrith Road
Castlerigg Manor (Catholic Youth Centre) Ambleside Road
Castlerigg Manor Lodge Ambleside Road
8 Main Street (formerly Central Hotel)
2 & 2a Chestnut Hill House Shelley Cottage with Adjoining Stables and Coach House to North

1 Penrith Road (formerly County Hotel)
St Herberts Centre (formerly Crosthwaite Sunday School)
Crosthwaite Vicarage Vicarage Hill
Derwent Isle House on Derwentwater Island
Dog and Gun Public House Lake Road
Forge Bridge Forge Lane
George Hotel St John's Street
Heads House Main Street
Ivy Cottage High Hill
Keswick School of Industrial Arts High Hill
Keswick Railway Station Building and Platform Station Road
King's Arms Hotel Market Square
Oak Cottage, Oak Lodge Ambleside Road
33 Lake Road (Formerly Mayson's Shop)
Oddfellows Arms Public House Main Street
Old Chapel at Landing Stage on Derwentwater Island
Old Windebrowe Brundholme Road
Packhorse Inn Including Attached Former Stables Packhorse Court
The Chief Justice Of The Common Pleas (former Police Station and Magistrates Court) Bell Close/Bank St
Priorholm Hotel 9 Borrowdale Road,
Royal Oak Hotel Station Street,
Ruskin Monument Friars' Crag, Lake Road
Skiddaw Cottage Vicarage Hill,
Small Outbuilding Opposite Packhorse Inn and Behind Ye Olde Friars Main Street, Keswick, Cumbria
Toll Bar Cottage Chestnut Hill

A Short History of Keswick

Evidence for the history of Keswick goes back to Neolithic times. Stone implements and weapons have been found at Portinscale and the 5000-year-old Castlerigg Stone Circle is evidence of early occupation, though no-one knows exactly why it was built.

The Romans had camps nearby. St Kentigern and St Herbert came in the sixth and seventh centuries and place names with elements like 'thwaite', 'seat' and 'dale' confirm settlement by the Norsemen from approximately the ninth century. In 1276, Edward I granted the town its market charter (the name 'Keswick' may mean 'cheese farm') and the Saturday market continues to this day.

The rural economy, based on wool, leather and farm products, was transformed in the reign of Elizabeth I. German miners exploited the rich minerals, copper in particular, of Newlands and Borrowdale. The discovery of graphite at Seathwaite in the sixteenth century sparked off pencil making which was a major industry in the town until 2008.

Tourism is now the major industry for Keswick, growing from a small number of privileged early visitors in the late 1700s and early 1800s – often attracted by Keswick's close association with the Romantic poets Southey, Coleridge and Wordsworth – to the rapid expansion in tourism brought about by the opening of the Cockermouth, Keswick and Penrith Railway to passenger traffic in 1865. The town expanded to meet the growing demands of visitors, and in the 1970s the construction of the M6 brought a new influx of car-borne tourists. Today lots of different challenging outdoor activities, events and festivals, as well as the spectacular environment, attract a wide range of people to Keswick.

Illustration: Engraving by J. B. Pyne.
The Vale of Keswick, Bassenthwaite, Lakeland, The River Greta.
Published 1853. From Keswick Museum collection.

Further Reading:

Armstrong, Margaret: *Linen and Liturgy: The Story of the Marshall Family and the Parish Church of Keswick St John*
Peel Wyke, 2002

Bott, George: *Keswick: The Story of a Lake District Town*
Bookcase, 1994

Bowtell, Harold D.: *Rails Through Lakeland: Illustrated History of the Workington, Cockermouth, Keswick, Penrith Railway*
Silver Link Publishing 1996

Bruce, Ian: *The Loving Eye and Skilful Hand: The Keswick School of Industrial Arts*
Bookcase, 2001

Fletcher Smith, Thomas: *Jonathan Otley - Man of Lakeland*
Bookcase, 2007

Foot, Elizabeth & Howell, Patricia: *Keswick Characters: 1, 2 & 3*
Bookcase, Oct 2006-9

Gamles, Robert: *Escape to the Lakes - The First Tourists*
Bookcase, 2012

Hankinson, Alan: *The Blue Box - The Story of the Century Theatre 1947-1983*
Bookcase, 2009

Hyde, Matthew and Pevsner, Nikolaus: *The Buildings of England: Cumbria*
Yale, 2010

Hyde, Matthew and Whittaker, illustrated by Val Corbett :
Arts and Crafts Houses in the Lake District
Frances Lincoln, 2014

Murray, John R.: A *Tour of the English Lakes: with Thomas Gray and Joseph Farington RA*
Frances Lincoln, 2011

Powell, Cecilia and Hebron, Stephen: *Savage Grandeur and Noblest thoughts*
The Wordsworth Trust, 2010

Roberts, Ros: *Keswick Painting*
Bookcase, 2015

Thompson Ian: *The English Lakes A History*
Bloomsbury, 2010

Back Cover: First Ordnance Survey Map for Keswick from 1860s.
Courtesy of the Cumbria Archives Centre, Lady Gillford's House, Carlisle.